Teaching with Robert Munsch Books Vol. 3

Amy von Heyking

and

Janet McConaghy

Scholastic Canada Ltd.
Toronto New York London Auckland Sydney
Mexico City New Delhi Hong Kong Buenos Aires

We thank the students who provided questions for Robert Munsch,
and the parents who kindly shared their children's photographs.

Library and Archives Canada Cataloguing in Publication
Von Heyking, Amy J. (Amy Jeanette), 1965-
Teaching with Robert Munsch books / Amy von Heyking, Janet McConaghy.
ISBN-10: 0-439-97433-X (v. 1).-ISBN-10: 0-439-95702-8 (v. 2).—
ISBN-13: 978-0-545-99902-1 (v. 3)

1. Munsch, Robert N., 1945- —Study and teaching (Elementary)
2. English language—Study and teaching (Elementary)   3. Language arts
(Elementary)
4. Children's stories, Canadian (English)—Study and teaching (Elementary)
I. McConaghy, Janet II. Title.

PS8576.U575Z92 2003   C813'.54   C2003-901055-4

Cover and interior design by Andrea Casault
Cover illustrations copyright © by Michael Martchenko
Interior illustrations copyright © by Alan and Lea Daniel, Janet Wilson
and Michael Martchenko

6 5 4 3 2 1   Printed in Canada   07 08 09 10 11

Table of Contents

The Story of Robert Munsch

Who is Robert Munsch? He's one of North America's best-loved storytellers, and his books, including the best-selling *Love You Forever*, have been entertaining children for decades.

Robert grew up in a family of nine kids. You might think that would be pretty hard, but he says it was a good thing. He could do the things he liked — like reading — without much interruption. When Robert was younger, he was a "reading freak" and would read anything he could. His favourite book was *The Five Hundred Hats of Bartholomew Cubbins* by Dr. Seuss. He also liked to write poems — funny ones, of course.

It might be hard to believe, but Robert wasn't always a writer. He was working at a daycare centre when his boss's wife, a children's librarian, heard him telling stories. She thought the stories were very good, and told him he should write them down and send them to a publisher.

Can you imagine: nine publishers turned down his stories! Finally one publisher said yes, and that very first Robert Munsch book, *Mud Puddle*, came out in 1979. Even so, it was another five years before Robert finally quit his job at the daycare centre. Since then he has published more than fifty books!

Where does Robert get his ideas? They almost always come from kids. Sometimes he'll see someone in the audience when he is doing a storytelling and ask if they would like to be a character in one of the stories. Other times, he'll be inspired by a kid he meets or by a letter someone sends to him. Just about anything can give him an idea. But not all of his stories become books — there are just too many! When he does a storytelling session, he might tell fourteen or fifteen stories, most of them new. But sometimes one story seems stronger than the rest, so he'll take that one and tell it over and over again — sometimes for years. And one day he might decide that the story is ready to become a book.

It's important to Robert that his books can be enjoyed by kids regardless of where they live in North America, or even the world. So if a story is set in Toronto, he wants kids in the Northwest Territories to enjoy it just as much as ones who live in the city, and vice versa. It can be a real trick to get the stories to work out so kids everywhere can relate to them.

Robert likes telling stories in schools and libraries. Sometimes, if he's going to be in a particular area, he'll check to see if a local school has written to him. Then he'll pay them a surprise visit. Sometimes he'll call a library or school and ask them to find an interesting family that he can stay with when he is travelling. Lucky them!

What does Robert do for fun? He likes to read, take his dogs for walks outside of town, ride his bicycle and even climb trees! And he loves to eat "hot, hot chicken wings."

Robert has three children, Julie, Andrew and Tyya, and he's written stories for all of them. The family in *Andrew's Loose Tooth* is Robert Munsch's — or Michael Martchenko's version of them, anyway.

Robert also keeps busy by reading and responding to the letters he gets. Each month he gets about 200 letters from schools and another 200 from individual children. That's a lot of reading and writing to catch up on!

Being a good storyteller is something that Robert has been blessed with. Still, it took him a long time to realize that he was pretty good at it. He often wonders exactly what it is that makes a person a great storyteller. Being able to think on your feet is part of it, but it's also really important to be a good listener — especially when it comes to listening to children. Of course, he's so good at telling stories that it's made him popular with children the world over.

Being a writer takes dedication as well as talent, but as Robert says, "This is the best job I've ever had."

From *Munsch More!: A Robert Munsch Collection*

Munsch Merits

Some parents may express concern about the "tone" of Munsch books. Emphasize that:

- the humour comes from exaggeration, which has great appeal for children.

- the stories take a zany approach to familiar childhood experiences; they are fantasy, and children understand this.

- the humour often depends on situations where children get the better of their parents or other authority figures. This kind of role reversal is fun for children.

- children learn how the language and the illustrations combine to capture the playfulness of the stories.

Robert Munsch Q & A

Aaron's Hair

Q: "Why does Aaron's hair have eyes?"
Emily, 8 years old

A: "Aaron's hair has eyes because it is pretend-alive and it needed pretend eyes to be pretend-alive."

Q: "I think a good title for this story would be *The Runaway Hair* or *The Tortoise and the Hair*. How do you choose the titles for your stories?"
Jonas, 8 years old

A: "Figuring out the title of a story is the last thing that happens. It is hard to figure out what is best."

Q: "Do you like your hair? When I have a bad hair day, I just wear a hat. Did you ever have a bad hair day?"
Alison, 8 years old

A: "I almost never comb my hair and it is mostly a mess. My kids freak out."

Lighthouse

Q: "Why did you use a different illustrator than Michael Martchenko?"
Wrhett, 9 years old

A: "I changed illustrators for *Lighthouse* because it was not a funny book and I wanted it to look different."

Q: "What made you decide to write a more serious story?"
Rosaleigh, 8 years old

A: "I wrote *Lighthouse* because of a drawing a kid gave me. The story just fit the drawing."

Q: "Is there someone that you miss? How do you remember them?"
Selena, 8 years old

A: "I miss my great-aunt Hannah. She used to tell me stories."

No Clean Clothes

Q: "Why did you pick a bear to kiss Lacey at the end?"
Chance, 8 years old

A: "In Lacey's school in Stewart, British Columbia, bears often come onto the playground. If black bears come, the librarian chases them away with a broom. If grizzly bears come, the kids cannot go out for recess. On the day I made up *No Clean Clothes*, there were GRIZZLY BEARS on the playground."

Q: "Where did you get the idea to write Kiss Me — I'm Perfect on the shirt?"
Todd, 9 years old

A: "Lacey was wearing a real shirt that said Kiss Me — I'm Perfect. I did not make it up."

Q: "I have a shirt that says Sister for Sale. Do you have an embarrassing shirt?"
Noah, 8 years old

A: "When I was in Grade 2, my grandma gave me an embarrassing shirt that had a cute little bunny on it."

I'm So Embarrassed!

Q: "Did your mom ever embarrass you when you were little?"
Chaylynn, 8 years old

A: "Actually, it was my DAD who embarrassed me all the time. He used to pat me on the head like I was a little toddler, only I was 10 YEARS OLD. He would PAT ME ON THE HEAD while he talked to people at the MALL."

Q: "Why did you put a moose in your story?"
Syanne, 8 years old

A: "Andrew Livingstone, the kid in *I'm So Embarrassed!*, lives near Cobalt, Ontario. Cobalt is surrounded by a forest that is full of moose. I mean, like, really FULL of MOOSE."

Q: "Why did you pick a trash can to have Taylor-Jae and Andrew jump in?"
Alexandra, 8 years old

A: "I used the trash can because I wanted to jump in one when I was EMBARRASSED!"

Q: "Do you embarrass your kids? How?"
Emily, 8 years old

A: "I really, really, really, really, really embarrass my kids because I dress like a bum and tell very, very unfunny jokes and don't comb my hair and generally act sort of crazy."

More Pies!

Q: "What is your favourite kind of pie?"
Bryson, 8 years old

A: "My favourite pie is apple pie."

Q: "How do you come up with the 'sound' words in the story?"
Noah, 8 years old

A: "When I am telling stories I make lots of strange sounds. If they are not too strange, I try to spell them and use them in the book."

Q: "What kind of an eating contest would you win?"
Emma, 8 years old

A: "I think I would win a licorice-eating contest. The town where I live has a Dutch store that has almost 100 DIFFERENT KINDS of licorice. I am a licorice fiend!!!"

The Sandcastle Contest

Q: "How did Kalita make the dog come alive?"
Justin, 8 years old

A: "Kalita did not know how she made the sand dog alive. I think Kalita is magic and does not know that she is."

Q: "What would be your favourite contest prize?"
Devon, 8 years old

A: "My favourite prize would be a trip where I would go diving to look at lots of fish."

A Picture of Michael Martchenko

Michael Martchenko's art is well known to kids, parents and teachers across the country — and although he's illustrated books by lots of writers (including himself!), he is best known for his work with Robert Munsch.

Michael has always loved drawing. As a boy, he copied comic book covers, imitating the lines and colour. "It was great practice," he says. He was unable to take art classes in high school, but that didn't stop him. He still knew he wanted to be an artist, so he decided to study illustration at the Ontario College of Art in Toronto.

After graduating, Michael worked as a junior art director for an advertising company. His job was to work on storyboards, designing ads. That's where he thought he'd stay for the rest of his life. Then one day, at an art show, Robert saw Michael's work and was attracted to his lively style. He approached Michael to do the pictures for *The Paper Bag Princess*, and a terrific partnership was born.

At first, Michael didn't think much of the story. "My first reaction was 'Yuck!'" he says. He thought it was a typical fairy tale about a prince and princess. But then he read it and thought, "This is cool!"

But Michael didn't quit his advertising job at first. "I thought illustrating books was something I could do when I retired," he says. "I never thought about doing it full-time." So he would work during the day at the advertising agency, then spend the evenings and weekends working on his picture book illustrations.

Michael has now been creating picture books full-time for about ten years, and he couldn't be happier. "I love what I do," he says.

What's his secret to illustrating? When he first gets a story, Michael doesn't draw the sketches right away. Instead, he'll get what he calls "mind pictures" of what would work in the story. Then he'll do thumbnail sketches, or storyboards, just like he did when he was an art director. Full pencil drawings come next. Then the paintings are done in watercolours.

And what about the funny background images that his fans love? Well, he didn't always do them. As time went on, the ideas started to come to him. He didn't set out to have, say, an exotic bird watching TV on top of the fridge in

More Pies!. "They just happen," he says of the extra touches. Readers have come to expect them, but he believes that it's important to make sure that those background images aren't too distracting.

When he was doing the illustrations for *Mmm, Cookies!*, Michael started what has become a tradition in his books with Robert Munsch — he put in a pterodactyl. Robert liked it so much, he asked Michael to put it in all their books, and that's just what Michael does. (Look for it in four of the stories featured in this book.)

What does Michael like to do besides illustrate? He loves history and airplanes. In fact, he collects aviation material, like old uniforms and badges. He's created paintings of historical planes. He also recently picked up his guitar again. This helps him to relax a little from his busy schedule.

Michael Martchenko and Robert Munsch have developed a wonderful partnership, and their collaboration has brought great happiness to many people over the years. And, just as important, Michael has found great happiness himself.

"I still can't believe I'm doing this for a living," he says.

Adapted from *Munsch More!: A Robert Munsch Collection*

A Picture of Alan and Lea Daniel

Alan grew up in Belleville and Hamilton, Ontario, and has fond memories of bike riding and playing in the "swamp." He always had a love of books and his parents often took him to the library and read to him. He and his friends would act out their favourite stories.

Over the years he has had many interesting jobs: delivering newspapers, working on a farm, camp director. He didn't think about becoming an illustrator, however, until he met one while he was in university. His mentor encouraged him to draw and paint and helped him get some jobs making diagrams and maps for children's books. He hasn't stopped working since! Over the years he has illustrated the Cat Pack series by Phyllis Reynolds Naylor, James Howe's Bunnicula series, and many nonfiction books like Janet Lunn's *The Story of Canada* and *Eh? to Zed* by Kevin Major.

Alan does a lot of research in order to complete his illustrations, sometimes checking sources on the Internet, but often visiting libraries, museums and archives, talking to experts, and even travelling and taking photographs. He has used many different materials for his illustrations, including watercolour, gouache, acrylic and oil.

Alan and his wife Lea often share the work of illustrating books. They brainstorm together but divide responsibilities different ways depending on the job. Often, Alan sketches the initial ideas and does the drawings, and Lea does the painting. Sometimes they include details like their own furniture in their drawings, or use friends and family for inspiration for their drawings. The two boys in their book *Under a Prairie Sky*, written by Anne Laurel Carter, were based on their grandsons. The central character in *The Best Figure Skater in the Whole Wide World* by Linda Bailey was based on a neighbour.

The Daniels have illustrated three Robert Munsch books together — *Good Families Don't*, *Get Out of Bed!* and *Aaron's Hair*. Their bright and animated pictures are a wonderful complement to Munsch's wild stories. They say that the best part of illustrating Munsch's books is the fun they have doing it. The hardest part is keeping their silliness in check. They begin with photographs Robert Munsch provides of the children who inspired the story. They then visualize the story and draw the action from many different angles until they are satisfied they have found the best ones. Often, it helps to hear Robert Munsch tell the story several times, because each time they will hear and picture something different. Sometimes the visual ideas that they have lead to changes or additions in the text.

A Picture of Janet Wilson

Janet Wilson was born in Toronto and now lives in Eden Mills, Ontario. When she was young she enjoyed spending summers at a cottage in Muskoka that was filled with books. She always enjoyed drawing and painting, but never thought she was good enough to earn a living as an artist. Eventually she decided that she really wanted to learn to be a professional artist, so she went to the Ontario College of Art. The first children's book she illustrated was *Daniel's Dog* by Jo Ellen Bogart. Since then her beautiful and realistic illustrations have been featured in storybooks including *At Grandpa's Sugar Bush*, *Lighthouse: A Story of Remembrance* and *Selina and the Bear Paw Quilt*, which won the Elizabeth Mrazik-Cleaver Canadian Picture Book Award for best illustration. She has also illustrated nonfiction books such as *In Flanders Fields: The Story of the Poem by John McCrae* by Linda Granfield and *Imagine That!* which she wrote as well as illustrated.

In order to complete her illustrations, Janet reads the manuscript of the book very carefully. She does a lot of research about the subject of the book, looking up information in libraries and museums and searching for pictures. She might also travel and take photographs to help her remember details. After she has done her research, she often just lets herself dream or just lets the images "float" in her head. She says the best time to think about her work is just as she's going to sleep, or first thing when she wakes up!

Once she is ready to start her illustrations, she uses real people for models of the characters. All the research she has done — and her models — help her make her illustrations realistic and expressive. She uses different materials such as watercolours, pastels and sometimes oils for her illustrations.

AARON'S HAIR

Summary:

Aaron wants to have long hair like his father, but as it grows it flips up, down, over and under and drives him crazy. He hates his hair! His hair jumps off his head and leads Aaron on a chase all around the town and back to his house. It's only when Aaron decides he likes his hair after all that it jumps back on his head.

The story behind Aaron's Hair

This story was a long time in the making. Many years ago Aaron was a student in Robert Munsch's preschool class. He had long hair and it was often uncombed. Robert Munsch made up many stories for and about his young students, and this was one he wrote about Aaron's hair running away from him. Years later, when he and his editor were deciding which of his old stories might become good books, they found a version of this story. By that time Aaron was grown up, living in Toronto and playing in a rock band. It goes to show that sometimes good stories take years to grow, just like hair!

Questions:

Before

Look at the front cover.
- What do we know about Aaron's hair from looking at the cover?
- Why do you think there are combs in his hair?
- Make some predictions about what you think will happen in the story.

Look at the back cover.
- What information can we find out about the author and the illustrators?
- Read the description on the back of the book. What is a "bad hair day"?

Look at the dedication page.
   (Note: In this book it is the last page.)
- Robert Munsch was Aaron's preschool teacher in 1980. Check the publication date of the book. How old would Aaron be now? Why do you think Robert Munsch waited so long to write this book?
- What do you think the children of Guelph do to the statue?

During

- p. 2: Why does Aaron hate his hair? What do you think will happen next?
- p. 20: How do the people get rid of Aaron's hair?
- p. 24: Where is the hair? How is Aaron going to get his hair back?

After

- Why does Aaron like his hair at the end of the story?
- Check the predictions you made about the story. Were you correct?
- This story was twenty years old by the time it finally became a book. Are there any clues in the illustrations that this story is set in the past? Hint: check out the camera on page 1 and some of the fashions on pages 18 and 19.

Take a look

How are Alan and Lea Daniel's illustrations the same as or different than Michael Martchenko's? What kinds of things do the Daniels put in their illustrations to add humour to the story?

On the back cover it says that they often put their pets in their pictures. After looking carefully at the illustrations, what kinds of pets do you think the Daniels have?

Chasing Aaron's Hair

Curriculum Link:
Social Studies — mapping

Materials:
Templates of places in the story (see reproducible on page 13)

Procedure:
1. Tell students that this story includes a chase, so it is a good story to use to create a map — not a story map in the sense of identifying the major events in the plot, but a map showing Aaron's hair's route.

2. Review the story and identify all the places the hair goes. In some cases it is obvious, e.g. Aaron's home; in other cases children might need to look more closely at the illustrations to guess, e.g. the man is at a playground on pages 12-13. Ask students to note where the hair ends up, i.e. at home, the same place it started.

3. Explain to students that when a story ends at the same place it began, a circle map can be created to show the journey of an item or character.

4. Using cut-outs of the templates provided on the reproducible, ask students to create their own circle maps showing Aaron's hair's journey.

Extension:
◉ Children can create their own maps using one of the titles below.

Literature Connections:
Hurry Up, Franklin by Paulette Bourgeois,
    illustrated by Brenda Clark
Rosie's Walk by Pat Hutchins
The Gingerbread Man by Carol Jones
The Big Green Pocketbook by Candice Ransom,
    illustrated by Felicia Bond
We're Going on a Bear Hunt by Michael Rosen,
    illustrated by Helen Oxenbury

Places Templates

Enlarge templates to suit classroom use.

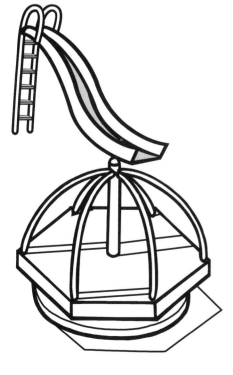

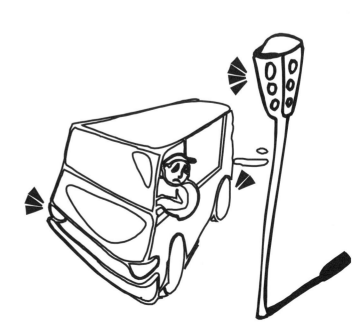

Activity #2

Wanted: Hair Control

Curriculum Link:
Language Arts

Materials:
Samples of print advertisements from newspapers, magazines
Chart paper, poster paper
Felt markers or crayons

Procedure:
1. Examine pages 2 and 3 of the story. Review what Aaron hates about his hair.

2. Brainstorm how Aaron might control his hair. What kinds of products might help him? Clips? Spray? Gel? A hat?

3. Tell the students they are going to create an advertisement for a product to control Aaron's hair.

4. Discuss what makes an advertisement effective. It probably is eye-catching in some way. It may be colourful or funny. It might feature a cute mascot. It identifies your problem or need. For example, for a hair product it might say: "Does your hair flip up? Flip down? Flip under? Flip over?" It explains the benefits of using the product. It might show happy people using it. It might use language in a clever way, e.g. with an alliterative name like "Megan's Magic Mousse" or with a rhyming slogan. It is trying to persuade you to buy the product.

5. Distribute some samples of advertisements from the newspaper or from magazines, particularly those aimed at children. Ask the students to identify those that are most effective and explain why. List the criteria for an effective ad on chart paper or on the board. (You might also ask if the students think the products are really as good as the ads make them out to be.)

6. Have each student create his or her own product and design an effective ad persuading Aaron to buy it. Final copies should be drawn on chart paper with felt pens or crayons.

7. Have students share their ads with the class.

Extensions:

- Students could create radio ads or TV commercials rather than print ads.
- Talk about how advertisements are designed to make us want to buy products, and how sometimes the products are not really as good as the ads make them seem. Read *Arthur's TV Trouble* and discuss any experiences they have had with products, like toys, not living up to their advertisement.

Literature Connections:

Arthur's TV Trouble by Marc Brown

Top Three About Me

Curriculum Link:
Health

Materials:
Class set of Top Three About Me organizers (see reproducible on page 17)

Procedure:
1. Discuss with the students why Aaron got frustrated with his hair. Talk about reasons why he came to like his hair by the end of the story.

2. As a class, brainstorm things that make people unique: physical characteristics like the colour of their hair, personal qualities like a great sense of humour, or abilities like being a great skater. To spark some ideas, you might want to share one of the picture books listed below that celebrate children's individuality or identity.

3. Discuss with the children all the things that make them proud of themselves, inside and out. Have them identify which are the most important to them and why.

4. Distribute the Top Three About Me organizers and have students complete them and share them. Encourage them to add illustrations or other personal touches if they would like to do so.

Extensions:
◉ Organize a "Strange Hair Day" in the classroom, where everyone comes to school with strange hair.

◉ Compare and contrast the story *Aaron's Hair* with one of the self-awareness books listed below.

Literature Connections:
Incredible Me by Kathi Appelt, illustrated by G. Brian Karas
I Like Myself by Karen Beaumont, illustrated by David Catrow
Marvelous Me: Inside and Out by Lisa Bullard, illustrated by Brian Reibeling
I Like Me by Nancy L. Carlson
Hooray for You by Marianne Richmond
    Specifically about hair:
Wanda and the Wild Hair by Barbara Azore, illustrated by Georgia Graham
Little Toby and the Big Hair by Kim and Eugenie Fernandes
Happy to Be Nappy by bell hooks, illustrated by Chris Raschka
Crazy Hair Day by Barney Saltzberg

Top Three About Me

Name: _____

LIGHTHOUSE

Summary:

One night Sarah wakes up her father and asks him to take her to a lighthouse that was special to her grandfather. They leave quietly and drive through the town, stopping for doughnuts and coffee. They continue their journey and arrive at the lighthouse. Though the doors have always been locked in the past, tonight they find them open, so Sarah and her father enter and climb to the top. There they think about her grandfather who has recently died, and toss a flower down into the sea. As they return home, Sarah knows that one day she will continue the tradition by taking her own child to the lighthouse.

Questions:

Before

Tell the students you are going to read a story by Robert Munsch. Ask them what they expect from a Munsch story.

Look at the front cover.
- Do you think this is going to be a funny book? Why or why not?
- What do you notice about the cover illustration? How is it different or similar to the pictures that illustrators usually draw for Munsch books?
- Why would Robert Munsch be described as "the author of *Love You Forever*" rather than of *Aaron's Hair* or *No Clean Clothes*?
- What is "A Story of Remembrance"? Have you ever done something special to remember someone?
- Where in Canada do you think this story takes place?
- Make some predictions about the story and record them on chart paper.

Look at the back cover.
- Who is the illustrator for this book? Why would it say that she is "known for her sensitive, realistic paintings"? Does that give you any clues about what kind of story this might be?
- Read the description on the back of the book. What do you think Sarah and her father are going to remember?

Read the dedication page.
- To whom is this book dedicated?
- Where does she live? Was that one of the places you thought the story would be set in?
- Why do think the illustrator used models for her pictures?

During

- p. 16: Is the door going to open?
- p. 20: Can her grandpa hear her?

After

- Check the predictions you made about the story. Were you correct?
- Were you surprised at this story? Why or why not?
- Why do they do things the way Sarah's father and grandfather used to?
- Why does she throw the flower in the ocean?
- Who is in the photograph beside Sarah's bed (on the last page)?

Encourage students to listen to Robert Munsch read the story. (It is available on his website at www.robertmunsch.com). Talk about how he reads the story differently than most of his other stories.

Take a look

⊘ Why might Robert Munsch have used a different illustrator for this book?

⊘ How do Janet Wilson's illustrations help tell the story? How are they different than the usual illustrations of Munsch stories?

⊘ Most Munsch stories are illustrated with watercolour pictures. These illustrations were painted in oils on canvas. How does that change the look and feel of the story? Look at the illustrations on pages 6 and 7 and on pages 14 and 15 to appreciate the effect Janet Wilson created with the fog and the water.

My Special Place

Curriculum Link:
Language Arts

Procedure:
1. Discuss with the students why the story is called *Lighthouse*. Why is the lighthouse a special place for Sarah and her father?

2. Ask children if there are special places they visit with parents or by themselves. What makes these places special? Read one of the books suggested below for other examples of special places.

3. Tell the students they are going to write about their own special places, real or imagined. Brainstorm questions for information they might include, e.g. What is your place like? Is it indoors or outdoors? Do you visit your place with a family member, with a friend or by yourself? What kinds of things do you like to think about or do there? List their suggestions on chart paper.

4. After students have completed a first draft of their description, ask them to exchange it with a peer. Ask the peer to review the writing and then create five questions that will help the writer add more description and detail. Reviewing "question words" (where, what, when, who, why, how) might help students generate good questions to ask. Students might also check the list on the chart paper for ideas.

5. Ask the writers to review the questions their friends asked them. Have them incorporate their answers in the next draft of their description of their special place.

Extension:
◉ Children could draw an illustration of their special place, or even draw a map showing how to get there.

Literature Connections:
Where Is Grandpa? by T.A. Barron, illustrated by Chris K. Soentpiet
Secret Place by Eve Bunting, illustrated by Ted Rand
Secret Dawn by Edith Newlin Chase, illustrated by Yolaine Lefebvre
The Grandad Tree by Trish Cooke, illustrated by Sharon Wilson
All the Places to Love by Patricia MacLachlan, illustrated by Mike Wimmer
When I Was Young in the Mountains by Cynthia Rylant, illustrated by Diane Goode
A Quiet Place by Douglas Wood, illustrated by Dan Andreasen

Sharing Traditions, Changing Traditions

Curriculum Link:
Language Arts, Social Studies

Materials:
2 class sets of Venn diagrams (see reproducible on p. 23), and 1 set of T-charts (not provided)

Procedure:
1. Ask the students why Sarah and her father went to the lighthouse. Introduce the term "tradition," if the children themselves do not. Talk about traditions in their families that have been passed down from generation to generation.

2. Ask them if Sarah and her father did exactly the same things as her father and grandfather did when they visited the lighthouse. Can they recall anything that Sarah and her father did differently? Record their suggestions on chart paper.

3. Read the story again, and ask students to listen particularly for comments about how Sarah and her father did things the same way and differently than her father and grandfather.

4. After the reading, create a T-chart on the board. One column should have the heading, "Same," and the other, "Different." Under the "Same" heading, list all the things that Sarah and her father did the same as her father and grandfather, e.g. they got up in the middle of the night, they drove to the lighthouse. Under the "Different" heading, list all the things that Sarah and her father did differently, e.g. they stopped at the doughnut shop, they went to the top of the lighthouse.

5. Ask students to discuss why the tradition changed over time. Why weren't there any doughnut shops when Sarah's father was young? Why might the lighthouse door be open now? You might make connections to some of the children's family traditions and how those have changed over time.

6. When the chart is complete, explain that a Venn diagram is a visual organizer that we can use to compare and contrast things, to help us show how things are the same and different. Distribute the Venn diagram reproducible and demonstrate how to use it by filling it in using the information on the T-chart. Complete the bottom section that asks them to explain why the tradition changed over time.

7. Distribute a blank T-chart and another blank copy of the Venn diagram. Ask students to complete the T-chart with information about one of their own family traditions. Check their charts and then ask them to transfer that information to their Venn diagrams. Again, make sure they are challenged to think about why the tradition has changed over time.

Extensions:

◎ Ask students to predict how Sarah's visit to the lighthouse with her child in the future will be the same and different than her visit with her father.

◎ Ask students to identify how their family traditions might change over time and why.

Literature Connections:

The Grandad Tree by Trish Cooke, illustrated by Sharon Wilson
The Sugaring-off Party by Jonathan London, illustrated by Gilles Pelletier
Henry's First-Moon Birthday by Lenore Look, illustrated by Yumi Heo
Waiting for the Whales by Sheryl MacFarlane, illustrated by Ron Lightburn
Aiko's Flowers by Rui Umezawa, illustrated by Yuji Ando
Firedancers by Jan Bourdeau Waboose, illustrated by C.J. Taylor
Morning on the Lake by Jan Bourdeau Waboose, illustrated by Karen Reczuch

Name: _____

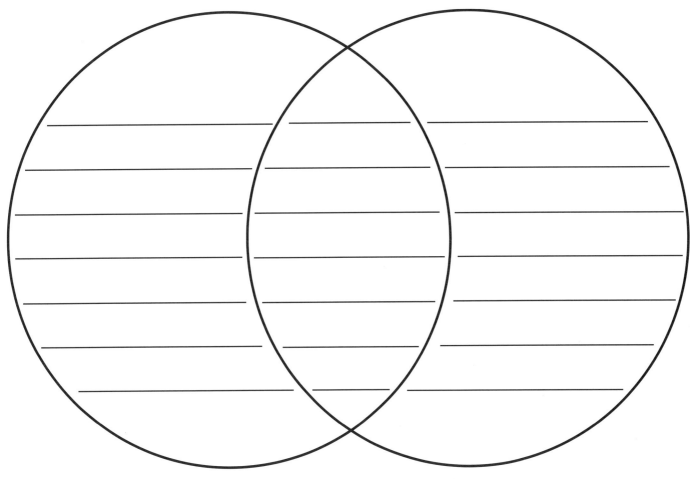

Why did it change?

Making a Memory Box

Curriculum Link:
Social Studies

Materials:
Teacher's own memory box, found boxes

Procedure:
1. Ask the students if they have ever made a scrapbook or if they have a special memory box. Why do we make scrapbooks? What might a "memory box" be?

2. Share your own memory box with the children. Your box should include objects that represent important people and events in your life. Tell the students the stories behind the objects and the memories they evoke.

3. Ask students to think about the ways Sarah and her father remember her grandfather. What do they do? Where do they go? Are there special objects that remind Sarah of her grandfather?

4. Tell students that you are going to read the story again, and this time when they listen to it, they are going to think of objects that Sarah might put in a memory box in order to remember her grandfather and the special trip to the lighthouse.

5. After your reading, create a list of the objects Sarah might include in her box. Ask children to explain why they have suggested the items listed. Items might include a pressed flower, a coffee cup or doughnut bag, a pebble Sarah might pick up on the path up to the lighthouse, and so on.

6. You might share some of the books listed below to talk more about memories and the objects that can spark memories.

7. Tell students they are going to create their own memory boxes. At home they can find an empty box and include in it any object that represents an important memory for them about people or places in their lives.

8. Give students the opportunity to share their memory boxes in the weeks that follow, allowing ample time for sharing and discussion.

Extension:

@ Students could choose one special object from their box to leave in a classroom museum. They should complete a label for their object that includes information about the item such as: name, current owner, materials it is made out of, date and place of origin, purpose, and its significance. They might leave a drawing or photo of the object rather than the actual object if it is particularly valuable to them.

Literature Connections:

The Memory Box by Mary Bahr, illustrated by David Cunningham
Oma's Quilt by Paulette Bourgeois, illustrated by Stéphane Jorisch
Wilfrid Gordon McDonald Partridge by Mem Fox, illustrated by Julie Vivas
Laura Charlotte by Kathryn O. Galbraith, illustrated by Floyd Cooper
A Box of Friends by Pam Muñoz Ryan, illustrated by Mary Whyte

The story behind No Clean Clothes

In 1988 Scholastic Canada held a contest and Robert Munsch was the prize! A Grade 2 class in Stewart, British Columbia, won, so Robert Munsch came to visit and stayed with two families in the community. One day when he was at the school for a reading, a girl named Lacey came to school wearing a T-shirt that said, "Kiss me – I'm perfect." Stewart is a pretty isolated community with lots of wildlife, and that day the children at the school could not go out for recess because there were three grizzly bears on the playground. Robert Munsch made up the story about all the animals kissing Lacey because of her T-shirt. Lacey is now a teenager and jokes that the story should be rewritten, as now she doesn't like the animal kisses and DOES like the boy kisses.

NO CLEAN CLOTHES

Summary:

When Lacey gets ready for school one morning, she discovers she has no clean clothes, except the embarrassing shirt her grandmother gave her for her birthday. So Lacey has to wear a shirt that says, "Kiss me — I'm perfect." As she walks to school, several animals read her shirt and give her a kiss, including a cat, a dog and an eagle. But even the moose kiss is better than the kiss she gets from Johnny! At recess, when Lacey is kissed by a bear, she and her classmates decide that her shirt is pretty cool. They order a bunch of embarrassing shirts from her grandmother.

Questions:

Before

Look at the front cover.
- What problem does the girl have?
- What do we know (or what can we predict) about the main character from the front cover?
- Does your room look like this?

Look at the back cover.
- What information can we find out about the author and the illustrator?
- What is the name of the child in the story?
- Read the description of the story. What kind of shirt could be weird or embarrassing? Have you ever had a shirt like that?

Look at the dedication page.
- Find Stewart, British Columbia, on a map of Canada. Do you think there could be grizzly bears there? What other animals do you think children there would see? On the back cover it says that there are no moose, eagles or bears in Michael Martchenko's backyard. What other differences might there be between Stewart and Toronto? How would life in Stewart be different or the same as in your community?

During

- p. 6: What do you think her shirt will say?
- p. 10: What is Lacey's mother's job?
- p. 14: What animal do you think will kiss Lacey next?
- p. 20: What will happen when Lacey wears her shirt in class?
- p. 22: What kisses Lacey at recess?
- p. 26: Do you think Lacey's grandma lives in the same community? Why or why not?

After

- Why does Lacey like her shirt at the end of the story?
- Why do all the children order strange grandma shirts? Would you?

Take a look

- How do Michael Martchenko's illustrations add to the humour of the story?

- Can you find Martchenko's signature pterodactyl?

- Do Lacey and her grandma live in the same city? How do we know? Look for clues in the illustrations on the last two pages.

Design Your Own Strange Grandma Shirt

Curriculum Link:

Art

Materials:

Class set of shirt outlines (see reproducible on p. 29)

Procedure:

1. Review the embarrassing T-shirts that Lacey has received from her grandma (refer to page 6 of the story). Ask the class why her Grandma would buy shirts like this for her granddaughter.

2. Discuss whether the children have ever received or worn T-shirts with weird or embarrassing sayings on them.

3. Talk about what designs might have been on the shirts Lacey received. Create a new design together for the "Kiss me — I'm perfect" shirt that Lacey wears in the story. Remember that on T-shirts, a clear, simple design is most effective, so share some examples of T-shirts with eye-catching designs and discuss what makes them work.

4. Tell the students they are going to have a chance to design their own weird T-shirt. The shirt should have a saying and a design.

5. Give students the shirt outline reproducible to complete their own weird T-shirt. Encourage them to share and post their work.

Extensions:

◎ The students' creations could be transferred to white T-shirts with magic markers or writing paint.

◎ Students could vote for their favourite design. The winner could be used for an iron-on that could be transferred onto T-shirts for the whole class.

Name: _____

My Strange T-Shirt Design

A Thank-You Letter for Grandma

Curriculum Link:
Language Arts

Materials:
Class set of friendly-letter organizers (see reproducible on p. 31)

Procedure:
1. Ask students what gifts they have received from their grandparents or other relatives. Talk about how they thank people for gifts. Do they write thank-you cards?

2. Tell the students that they are going to write Lacey's thank-you letter to Grandma for the shirt. The letter should say thank you, but should also include at least two things that Lacey likes about the shirt. Brainstorm what she might say, e.g. "I like the way the cat kissed me," or "It tells people how much you love me." You might also brainstorm other information that Lacey could include: the weather, greetings from her mother, etc. Record their ideas on chart paper or the board.

3. Distribute the friendly-letter organizers. Introduce students to the elements of a friendly letter: heading (usually just the date), salutation, body, conclusion and signature. Have students write a draft of their letter on the organizer page, using the brainstormed ideas to guide their writing.

Extensions:
- Have students write thank-you letters to parents or other relatives for gifts or kind gestures, or to Robert Munsch for writing such funny books!
- Have students write other friendly letters, using the picture books listed below to spark ideas.

Literature Connections:
With Love, Little Red Hen by Alma Flor Ada, illustrated by Leslie Tryon
Dear Annie by Judith Caseley
Dear Tooth Fairy by Alan Durant, illustrated by Vanessa Cabban
School Lunch by True Kelley
Dear Mrs. LaRue by Mark Teague

_____

(heading)

Dear _____

(salutation)

_____

(body)

_____

_____

_____

_____

_____

_____

_____

(conclusion)

_____

_____

_____

(signature)

Problem-Solving

Curriculum Link:
Language Arts, Social Studies

Materials:
Problem-solving organizers (see reproducible on p. 33)

Procedure:
1. Ask the children to identify Lacey's problem at the beginning of the story. Discuss why she does not have any clean clothes to wear to school (refer to page 4 of the story). Discuss whose responsibility it is for Lacey to have clean clothes. Is it fair for Lacey to blame her mother?

2. Write the problem — Lacey needs clean clothes, or Lacey needs to organize her room — in the appropriate box in the problem-solving organizer.

3. Brainstorm with the children as many different solutions to the problem as they can think of. For each solution, identify what might happen if that solution is put into action. For example, if Lacey put her clothes into a laundry hamper in her room, her mother would be able to find them and wash them.

4. Of all the possible solutions suggested, have students select the best option and explain why it is the best.

Extension:

◎ Brainstorm other typical daily problems the children face: doing household chores, completing homework, resolving disagreements with siblings. In pairs, have students select one problem, brainstorm solutions and select the best solution, recording their thinking on the organizer. Ask them to present their problems and their solutions to their peers.

Literature Connections:
When Mom Turned Into a Monster
   by Joanna Harrison
Please Clean Up Your Room!
   by Itah Sadu, illustrated by Roy Condy
Martin by Himself by Gloria Skurzynski, illustrated
   by Lynn Munsinger
Super-completely and Totally the Messiest
   by Judith Viorst, illustrated by Robin Preiss Glasser
Fritz and the Mess Fairy by Rosemary Wells

Name: _____

Problem-Solving Organizer

Problem: _____
_____
_____

Solution 1:
_____
_____
_____
_____
_____

Solution 2:
_____
_____
_____
_____
_____

Solution 3:
_____
_____
_____
_____
_____

What will happen?
_____
_____
_____
_____

What will happen?
_____
_____
_____
_____

What will happen?
_____
_____
_____
_____

The best solution: _____
_____
_____

I'M SO EMBARRASSED!

Summary:

Andrew desperately needs some new shoes but his mother always seems to embarrass him every time they go to the mall. Shortly after his mother promises not to embarrass him again, they enter a shopping mall — where in front of everyone, she spits on her hand to smooth down his hair. After running into Andrew's teacher, his mother pulls out Andrew's baby pictures to show him. Then Andrew meets his friend Taylor-Jae, who seems to have the same problem with her mother. The two children decide to make a plan. They announce to everyone in the mall that not only do their mothers snore like bears, but they blame it on their fathers. Now the mothers are the ones who are embarrassed!

Questions:

Before

Look at the front cover.
- Why do you think the boy has two red lip prints on his face?
- Can you think of another word that means the same as "embarrassed"?
- Can you think of a time that you have been embarrassed? Do you remember how you felt?

Look at the back cover.
- Read the description on the back of the book. What do you think Andrew and Taylor-Jae's plan will be? Record the students' predictions on a chart.
- The description on the back says that Andrew's mom is always embarrassing him. What are some of the ways you think she might embarrass him? Record the students' predictions on a chart.

Look at the dedication page.
- Sometimes an important image is used on the dedication page to tell us the main idea of the story. What do you think this image might mean?

- p. 2: Do you think Andrew's mom will keep her promise not to embarrass Andrew?
- p. 20: What do you think Taylor-Jae's mom is going to do?
- p. 28: What do you think Andrew and Taylor-Jae meant when they said, "We had good teachers!"?

After

- Check the predictions you made before reading the book.

Take a look

🌀 How many characters from other Robert Munsch books can you find in this story? Can you name them?

I'm a Cartoonist

In this activity the students will create a comic strip to retell the sequence of events in the story.

Curriculum Link:
Language Arts — retelling, sequencing
Art

Materials:
Chart paper
Class set of blank comic strips (see reproducible on p. 37)

Procedure:

1. Review the book with the students in order to identify the sequence of events that were embarrassing to Andrew. On a chart, record how the story begins, the embarrassing incidents in the order they took place, and how the story ends. Number the incidents as you record them.

2. Tell the students that they are going to make a comic strip to retell the story of *I'm So Embarrassed!*. Explain to the students that the purpose of most comic strips is to tell a story through pictures and words. Share samples of comic strips you have brought in with the class. As you read them out, point out the speech balloons and any written captions underneath.

3. Provide each student with a copy of the template to create a comic strip. Referring back to the chart, ask students to illustrate the beginning in box 1 of their comic strip. Then have them select 3 embarrassing incidents to illustrate in boxes 2, 3 and 4, and in the last box, have them illustrate the end of the story.

4. Have the students share their completed comic strips with their classmates in the Author's Chair.

Extensions:

◎ Students could create a class book of their individual cartoons.

◎ Reread pages 26 and 28 and ask the students to think of other endings that might have solved Andrew's problem.

Name: _____

Title: _____

Enlarge on 11" x 17" paper for classroom use.

Teaching with Robert Munsch Books, Vol. 3, p. 37 © 2007 Scholastic Canada Ltd.

My Most Embarrassing Moment

Curriculum Link:
Language Arts — writing about a personal experience

Materials:
Chart paper, journal

Procedure:
1. Begin by having the students recall some of the embarrassing moments for Andrew in the story *I'm So Embarrassed!*. Ask them why they think Andrew may have been embarrassed.

2. You may also want to share the book *My Grandmother Is a Singing Yaya* by Karen Scourby D'Arc.

3. With the students, discuss some embarrassing moments that have happened to them and record them on a chart.

4. Explain to the students that in their journals they are going to write about an embarrassing moment they experienced.

5. Begin by modelling an entry with the students, using a personal example or one from the chart. Show the students how they can add interesting details to their entries by asking themselves some questions. For example, where did this happen? When did this happen? How did they feel?

6. Invite students to share their entries in the Author's Chair.

Extension:
◎ Have the students write one or two sentences in their journal telling what the embarrassing moment was that they experienced. Then have them exchange their journal with a partner. Have their partner write five questions for them that would help them to elaborate on their ideas. You might want to review the Five Ws with the students (who, what, where, when, why) to help them with their questions.

Literature Connections:
Books to share with the students might include:
My Grandmother Is a Singing Yaya by Karen Scourby D'Arc, illustrated by
    Dianne Palmisciano
My Mother Talks to Trees by Doris Gove, illustrated by Marilynn H. Mallory

Dealing With Feelings

Curriculum Link:
Health — safe and appropriate ways for sharing and/or expressing feelings

Materials:
Chart paper
Class set of blank comic strips (see reproducible on p. 37)
Poster paper

Procedure:
1. Refer back to the pictures on pages 7 and 9. Ask the students if they think Andrew might be experiencing other feelings apart from being embarrassed.

2. Read aloud the story *When Sophie Gets Angry — Really, Really Angry* by Molly Bang. Discuss with the children what Sophie did when she was feeling really angry. Point out that Sophie handled her anger in a way that was safe and in which no one would be hurt.

3. On chart paper write the heading "angry" and brainstorm with the children what they do when they are feeling angry. Remind them that it is important to deal with emotions in ways that are safe and appropriate. Record their ideas on the chart.

4. Ask the students to tell you about some other feelings they may have experienced, e.g. disappointment, rejection, happiness. Under each heading list their ideas of how they might deal with these feelings.

5. Have the students select one of the "feelings" listed on the chart and create a cartoon with four or five panels showing what they would do when they are feeling this way. You may want to model one for the students.

Extension:
◎ The students could create posters for "safe" ways to handle different feelings.

Literature Connections:
Books to share with students might include:
When Sophie Gets Angry — Really, Really Angry by Molly Bang
Lizzy's Ups and Downs by Jessica Harper, illustrated by Lindsay Harper DuPont
Sometimes I'm Bombaloo by Rachel Vail, illustrated by Yumi Heo

The story behind More Pies!

Robert Munsch first told the story of *More Pies!* at a childcare centre in Coos Bay, Oregon. He had no idea at that time that this story would become a book. The main character, Samuel, was not based on a real person, so when he decided to write the book he realized that he didn't have a picture of Samuel to send to Michael Martchenko. Then one day he received a fan letter from a little boy named Samuel, so he wrote back asking him if he would like to be in his book. It turned out that not only did Samuel appear in the book but so did his little brother.

MORE PIES!

Summary:

One morning Samuel wakes up really hungry. After eating a large salad bowl filled with cereal, four milk shakes, four stacks of pancakes and a fried chicken, Samuel is still hungry! When his mother refuses to give him seven more fried chickens, Samuel decides to take his brother's advice and enter a pie-eating contest. Even though Samuel's competition turns out to be a fireman, a lumberjack and a construction worker, he still manages to win first prize! After returning home Samuel discovers that his mother has made pies for lunch. The thought of another pie turns Samuel green. But Samuel's little brother is more than ready to enjoy some!

Questions:

Before

Look at the front cover.
- What do you notice about the lettering used in the title?
- Do you think this pie the boy is eating is real? Why or why not?
- What is your favourite kind of pie?

Look at the back cover.
- What information can we find out about the author and the illustrator?
- Who is the child in the story?
- Read the description on the back of the book. Have you ever entered a contest?
- Do you think Samuel will win the pie-eating contest? Why or why not? Have the students vote and record their prediction on a chart.

Look at the dedication page.
- Sometimes an important image is used on the dedication page to tell us the main idea of the story. What do you think this image might mean?
- Why do you think Robert Munsch dedicated this book to Samuel Or?

During

- p. 8: What do you think Samuel will do next?
- p. 16: Do you think the construction worker thought that Samuel could win the contest?
- p. 24: What do you think Samuel will do with the pie that he won? What do you think his mother will say when he comes home with this pie?
- p. 28: Do you think Samuel's little brother will win the next pie-eating contest? Why or why not?

After

- Check the prediction you made before reading the book.
- Have the students write a recipe for their favourite pie. It could be real or imaginary.
- Read the information about the author on the back of the book. Have the children write a letter to Robert Munsch. You could brainstorm questions they might like to ask and record them on chart paper.

Take a look

- Can you find other Robert Munsch books or characters from his other stories in the illustrations?

- On page 12 point out the pictures of Robert Munsch and Michael Martchenko in the newspaper. Ask the students why they think their pictures may be in the paper and what they think the newspaper article might be about.

- Point out the names on the bus on page 25.

Get Ready, Set, Go!

In this activity students will learn the importance of eating a healthy breakfast. They will have the opportunity to design a variety of breakfast menus using Canada's Food Guide to help them make healthy choices.

For a copy of Canada's Food Guide go to:
http://www.hc-sc.gc.ca/fn-an/food-guide-aliment/index_e.html

Curriculum Link:
Health

Materials:
Class set of breakfast menus (see reproducible on page 44)
Chart paper
Class set of Canada's Food Guide

Preparation:
Before you begin, divide a piece of chart paper into four columns and label each column with the four food groups: Grain Products, Vegetables and Fruit, Milk and Alternatives, and Meat and Alternatives.

Procedure:
1. Refer back to page 7 of *More Pies!* and ask the students if they think this looks like a healthy breakfast.

2. Ask the students to remember if they have ever heard their parents say "Breakfast is the most important meal of the day." Ask the students why they think their parents may have said this.

3. Explain to the students that one reason might be that eating breakfast is the "fuel" that they need to begin their day — just like you need to put gas in a car so that it will run.

4. Point out to the students other important reasons for eating a healthy breakfast. For example, children who eat breakfast are likely to concentrate better in school and are more likely to participate in physical activities.

5. Brainstorm what they might eat for breakfast and record each food item on the chart you prepared earlier.

6. Share copies of Canada's Food Guide with the students and discuss the importance of eating a balanced diet.

7. Explain to the children that they are going to create their own breakfast menu using Canada's Food Guide. The menu must include one item from each food group.

8. Give each student a copy of the menu reproducible and have them create two different breakfasts on their menus, using words or pictures. (Students could write the word or draw pictures of the food.)

9. When the students have completed their menus they could fold the paper in half and design a menu cover for a favourite restaurant on the front.

10. Have the students share their menus with their classmates.

Extensions:

◎ Bring in a variety of cereal boxes to share with the students. Have them design their own cereal box and write a radio advertisement to sell their cereal.

◎ Share other books with the students in which the characters eat breakfast. Identify the different types of food they are eating. You might want to start with the story of Goldilocks and the Three Bears.

Breakfast Menu #1

Grain Products	Vegetables and Fruit

Milk and Alternatives	Meat and Alternatives

Breakfast Menu #2

Grain Products	Vegetables and Fruit

Milk and Alternatives	Meat and Alternatives

Name: _____

My Favourite Pie

In this activity students will have the opportunity to collect and interpret data through a class survey. They will record the information they collect in the form of a pictograph.

Curriculum Link:
Math — data analysis

Materials:
Class set of survey charts (see reproducible on p. 47)
Class set of pictographs (see reproducible on p. 48)

Procedure:
1. Refer back to the front cover of the book *More Pies!*. Ask the students: What kind of pie do you think Samuel is eating? What do you think his favourite kind of pie might be?

2. Explain to the students how to take a class survey to find out their classmates' favourite kind of pie. Remind them that a survey is a way of finding out information by asking questions. Talk to them about some of the reasons we might take a survey. For example, a baker might want to know what kind of pie is the most popular so he can bake them to sell in his bakery.

3. Invite the students to participate in a class survey. Have them brainstorm different kinds of pies and record these on chart paper. Limit the number of choices to eight.

4. Distribute the survey charts and have the students record four kinds of pie on the left. Above, have them write their question, e.g. What is your favourite pie? Which kind of pie would you like for dessert? Provide the students with a class list to help them keep track of which classmates they have surveyed.

5. Talk to the students about how they will record their findings on the right, e.g. tally marks, check marks.

6. Once they have completed their surveys, use one of the surveys as a sample to demonstrate how they can organize their data into a pictograph. Explain to the students that they may need to use a scale of 2 (or 5) for their pictograph, since they have surveyed a large number of people. You may also want to brainstorm ideas for the picture, or icon, they could use on the right, e.g. smiley faces, pies, apples.

7. Once the pictographs are completed you may want to make an overhead of a few samples to use for some questions, like: What is the most popular pie? How many more students preferred one kind of pie over another kind of pie? How many students did you survey altogether?

Extensions:

◎ The students could write about this experience in their math journal, describing how they carried out the survey and what they learned about their classmates.

◎ As a special treat you might like to bring in the flavour of pie that seemed to be the most popular to share with the students.

Literature Connections:

Pie in the Sky
by Lois Ehlert

Name: _____

Survey Chart

Question: _____
_____

1.	
2.	
3.	
4.	

Pictograph

Title: _____

1.	
2.	
3.	
4.	

Scale: Each ——— means ——— pies

Name: _____

Read All About It!

In this activity students will have the opportunity to take on the role of a reporter and write a news article.

Curriculum Link:

Language Arts — writing

Materials:

A sample newspaper
Chart paper
Class set of Read All About It! (see reproducible on p. 51)

Procedure:

1. Look back at page 22 and draw the students' attention to the man taking a picture. Suggest that this could be a reporter covering the pie-eating contest for a newspaper or a TV news report.

2. Bring in a sample newspaper to share with the students. Discuss the layout of the paper with them, including the size and importance of the headlines. Point out that articles in the newspaper are often written in columns, and that sometimes a photograph of the journalist will be included.

3. Discuss how reporters cover special events and then write articles about them for the newspaper.

4. Tell the students that they are going to become a reporter and write an article about the pie-eating contest for their local newspaper.

5. Discuss with the students how reporters often use the Five Ws and How (Who, What, Where, When, Why) to help them write their news stories.

6. Brainstorm with the students questions they might have about the pie-eating contest. For example: When did the pie-eating contest take place? Where was the contest held? Who were the contestants? What was first prize? Record questions on a chart.

7. Model how to go about writing a news article using some of the questions from the chart as a sample.

8. Using the questions, have the students write their own news article. Explain to the students that the article can be imaginary and encourage them to think of details beyond the information found in the text and illustrations.

9. Have the students do a first draft for you to revise and edit.

10. Once the writing has been edited, have them write a good copy on the Read All About It! reproducible page and include a photo or illustration.

11. Have the students share their final copy with their classmates in the Author's Chair.

Extensions:

◎ Create a classroom newspaper to share with parents about important events in the classroom and school.

◎ Students could also make individual newspapers and include a variety of sections, e.g. City News, Classified Ads, Sports.

Read All About It!

_____

(headline)

_____

_____

Written by: _____

_____ _____

_____ _____

_____ _____

_____ _____

_____ _____

_____ _____

_____ _____

THE SANDCASTLE CONTEST

Summary:

When Matthew's family packs up their camper for their trip they take everything with them, including the kitchen sink. When Matthew arrives at the beach he enters a sandcastle-building contest. He meets Kalita, one of the contestants, and admires her sand dog. Matthew builds such an amazing sand house that he even fools the judges into believing that it is real. After Matthew proves to the judges that it is just made out of sand they declare him the winner! Then Kalita shows Matthew how to make a sand dog of his very own so that he can finally have the pet he always wanted.

Questions:

Before

Look at the front cover.
- Look at the expression on the little boy's face. What is he thinking at this very moment?
- Look at the flag on the small sandcastle. What country does that flag belong to?
- Why do you think the author chose a Canadian flag for the sandcastle?
- Have you ever built a sandcastle? Who helped you? Anyone?
- What does it mean to enter a contest?

Look at the dedication page.
- The illustration used on this page appears somewhere in the book. See if you can spot it as you are listening to the story.

Look at the back cover.
- Read the description on the back of the book. Describe a contest that you have entered.
- Why do you think Matthew might or might not win the sandcastle contest?
- Record the students' predictions on a chart.

- p. 2: Do you think Matthew's mother and father will get him a dog?
- p. 12: Why do you think Kalita would put a sand dog on a leash?
- p. 16: Why do you think the judges thought that this was a "real" house?
- p. 20: Do you think Matthew will still have a chance to win the contest after burying the judges in the sand?
- p. 24: How do you think Kalita turned her sand dog into a real dog?

After

- Check the predictions you made before reading the book.

Take a look

- Make sure the children have a chance to examine and enjoy the illustrations. In this story children should notice all the items Matthew's family took with them on their camping trip that "don't fit" — such as the kitchen sink, jack-o'-lantern and the skates.

- Point out to the students that many of the sand structures are world-famous landmarks. Ask them if they can name any of these landmarks. You might want to bring in photographs of the Eiffel Tower, the Taj Mahal and other famous structures to share with the students.

Design Your Own Sandcastle

In this activity students will have the opportunity to design their own sandcastle using simple clay-modelling techniques. Before the students begin building their sandcastles you might also want to share the book *Sand Castle* by Brenda Shannon Yee for more ideas.

Curriculum Link:
Art — modelling techniques, e.g. pinching, rolling, making coils
Language Arts — representing interesting or important aspects of a story

Materials:
Pictures of castles
Clay (self-hardening) or Plasticine
Modelling tools, e.g. toothpicks, popsicle sticks, plastic utensils
Tempera paint (a variety of colours)
Cardboard squares
Tinfoil
Chart paper
Book: *Sand Castle* by Brenda Shannon Yee

Preparation:
Before you begin, cut out a cardboard square for each student and cover it with tinfoil.

Procedure:
1. Refer back to the picture of the sandcastle on the front cover of the book *The Sandcastle Contest.*

2. Discuss with the students the different parts of a castle and the original purpose that these features served. For example, the moat around the castle was a security device.

3. You may want to record the parts of a castle on a chart as a reference when developing the criteria list of what the students will need for making their own sandcastles.

4. Show the children photographs of famous castles around the world.

5. Explain to the students that they are going to design their own castle using modelling clay.

6. Develop a criteria list (refer back to the chart) of the minimum requirements of what their castle should include, e.g. three towers, a moat, a drawbridge.

7. Before you begin, demonstrate some modelling techniques using the various tools with the students.

8. Have the students build their castle on the tinfoil-wrapped cardboard.

9. If you are using the self-hardening clay, allow it to dry overnight. The students could paint their castles once they are dry.

10. You might like to display the castles in the library once they are completed.

Extensions:

◎ Students can create their own sand paintings. Students begin by drawing a simple picture. Select one area to begin colouring and cover it with white glue. Sprinkle on coloured sand (sand mixed with powdered tempera paint) using a spoon. Use different colours for other areas, gently shaking off the excess. When the painting is finished, spray it with hair spray to fix the sand in place.

◎ Have the students make plaster of Paris relief sculptures.

Literature Connections:
Books to share with students might include:
Hamlet and the Magnificent Sandcastle by Brian Lies
A Really Good Snowman by Daniel J. Mahoney
Sand Castle by Brenda Shannon Yee, illustrated by Thea Kliros

From a Sand Dog to a Real Dog

The book *The Sandcastle Contest* shows Kalita with her sand dog on page 9. Then on page 13, Kalita's dog has become real. The author doesn't give an explanation as to how Kalita's dog goes from being a sand dog to a real dog. In this activity students will have the opportunity to add the missing information to the story.

Curriculum Link:
Language Arts — writing

Materials:
Chart paper
Student journals

Procedure:
1. Begin by rereading pages 8 to 12 of *The Sandcastle Contest* to the students.

2. Discuss with the students that the author doesn't offer any explanation as to how Kalita's dog becomes real.

3. Ask the students how they think it may have gone from being a sand dog to a real dog. Record their ideas on chart paper.

4. Explain to the students that they are going to write about how they think Kalita's dog came to life.

5. Begin modelling by orally elaborating on one of the ideas recorded on the chart.

6. Then have the students write a journal entry describing how they think Kalita's dog became real. They might want to select one of the ideas you brainstormed together to elaborate on for their entry.

7. Have the students share their entries with a partner.

Literature Connections:
Another book to share with students might be:
Sandmare by Helen Cooper, illustrated
   by Ted Dewan

Judging a Contest

Curriculum Link:
Language arts — recording ideas using a list

Materials:
Chart paper

Procedure:

1. Have the students recall a contest that they may have entered and how the judges decided who would win.

2. Ask the students if they know what the word "criteria" means. You may be already using criteria lists with your students in the classroom for assignments. (See sample below.) Explain to the students that for a contest there is sometimes a list of criteria that people must meet in order to win. Refer back to the picture on page 14 in *The Sandcastle Contest* and point out the clipboard that the judge is holding. Ask the students why they think the judge would need a clipboard.

CRITERIA FOR A SOCIAL STUDIES BOOKLET
Read each box and check the column that matches your work. If your work does not meet the criteria, decide what you need to do to improve it.

☺ ☺ ☹	My work meets the criteria. I need to do more work to meet the criteria. I have not met the criteria.	☺	☺	☹
I used my Social Studies textbook to find ideas.				
I have used complete sentences.				
My sentences have capitals and punctuation.				
My sentences contain details or specific examples that identify the country.				
I used my neatest printing.				
I have a neatly coloured picture for each country.				
My cover is filled in neatly.				

3. Tell the students that they are going to work with a partner to come up with a list of criteria that they would use if they were judges in this contest. For example, you must only use sand; you need at least two towers, etc.

4. After the students have completed their criteria lists, they could share them with a partner and determine some of the similarities and differences.

Extension:

◎ Together with the students, begin developing criteria lists for assignments.

Ideas for a Munsch Author Study

◎ Write and perform a Readers' Theatre production of your favourite Munsch book. Note: *More Pies!* works well.

◎ Make a puppet show with your favourite Munsch book.

◎ Design a book jacket for your favourite Robert Munsch book. The jackets could be laminated and displayed in a Munsch Corner in the classroom.

◎ Create a bookmark representing your favourite Munsch book. Choose a shape that reflects a character, building, or object in the book.

◎ Make character sketches for major characters in the Munsch books. What qualities do many of the main characters have in common?

◎ Use a shoebox or cardboard box to create a diorama of a scene from your favourite Robert Munsch book. Write a brief description about the book it came from, and which scene it represents. The dioramas and descriptions could be displayed in a glass case in the school.

◎ Create a Story Wheel of your favourite Robert Munsch book. Divide a circle into six to eight segments. Retell events of the story by moving clockwise around the circle.

◎ Make a Munsch Monument. Build a 3-D tribute to Munsch and include objects to represent the people or situations in his books. Explain what you included and why.

◎ Work with a partner to plan and create a mural of your favourite Robert Munsch book. The mural could centre on the events of a particular Robert Munsch book, or it could be a mural representing your favourite Munsch characters. Use a variety of media to create your mural. For example: paints, chalk, pastels, construction paper, cotton balls, chenille stems, coloured tissue, scraps of material.

◎ Have a special lunch and come as your favourite Munsch character. Call it A Meal for Munschkins. Remember to have cookies and pies for dessert!

◎ Write a story in the style of Robert Munsch. (Check Robert Munsch's website for some examples from other classes). Remember to include your favourite sound effects.

◎ Write a letter to Robert Munsch applying for a job as his assistant. Tell him why you would be a great candidate to help him do his job.

◎ Many of Munsch's stories are outlandish or crazy. Create your own crazy stories by brainstorming possible characters (names of people, animals, aliens), settings (the zoo, barnyard, home), and problems (running out of food, making too much noise) for stories. Have students write each character, setting, and problem idea they come up with on a separate slip of paper. Collect all the slips in three bags marked "Characters," "Setting," and "Problem." Pairs of students can then choose several slips from the character bag, one from the setting bag, and one from the problem bag. Ask them to work together to write a story using the characters and setting they drew, and resolving the problem they chose.

- Compare and contrast the zany Munsch books with his more serious books, like *Love You Forever*, *From Far Away* and *Lighthouse*.

- Listen to some of the stories on Robert Munsch's website. Are the stories he tells exactly the same as the stories in the books? Why or why not? What makes Robert Munsch such an effective storyteller? Practise retelling your favourite Munsch story.

- Many children and school classes write to Robert Munsch and try to convince him to come and visit. Look at some of the examples on his website, and then write your own letters and invitations trying to convince Robert Munsch to come visit your school.

- Make a commercial for a Munsch book.

- Write newspaper reviews of your favourite Munsch stories.

- After reading and responding to many Munsch books, ask students to consider why so many children enjoy Robert Munsch's stories. What do they expect when they prepare to listen to a Munsch story?

- Compare the books with some of the videos that have been made of Robert Munsch's stories.

- Invite parents or another class to a Munsch celebration. Children can read their favourite Munsch stories to parents or younger students, or tell their favourite stories aloud.

- A class at Denne Elementary School in Newmarket, Ontario, got dressed up and held their own class awards show. Have your class do the same, and give out Munschie Awards for:

- Best Major Character

- Best Animal Character

- Funniest Story

- Best Illustrations

- Favourite Story

LIST OF RESOURCES

Books by Robert Munsch

50 Below Zero
Aaron's Hair
Alligator Baby
Andrew's Loose Tooth
Angela's Airplane
Boo!
Boy in the Drawer, The
Class Clown
Dark, The
David's Father
Fire Station, The
From Far Away
Get Me Another One
Get Out of Bed!
Giant
Good Families Don't
I Have to Go!
I'm So Embarrassed!
Jonathan Cleaned Up – Then He Heard a Sound
Lighthouse: A Story of Remembrance
Love You Forever
Makeup Mess
Millicent and the Wind
Mmm, Cookies!
Moira's Birthday
More Pies!
Mortimer
Much More Munsch!
Mud Puddle
Munsch More!
Munschworks
Munschworks 2
Munschworks 3
Munschworks 4
Munschworks Grand Treasury, The
Murmel, Murmel, Murmel
No Clean Clothes
Paper Bag Princess, The
Pigs
Playhouse
Promise Is a Promise, A
Purple, Green and Yellow
Ribbon Rescue
Sandcastle Contest, The
Show and Tell
Smelly Socks
Something Good

Stephanie's Ponytail
Thomas' Snowsuit
Up, Up, Down
Wait and See
We Share Everything!
Where Is Gah-Ning?
Zoom!

Related Books

Aaron's Hair
Appelt, Kathi, illustrated by G. Brian Karas. (2002). Incredible Me
Azore, Barbara, illustrated by Georgia Graham. (2005). Wanda and the Wild Hair
Beaumont, Karen, illustrated by David Catrow. (2004). I Like Myself
Bourgeois, Paulette, illustrated by Brenda Clark. (1988). Hurry Up, Franklin
Brown, Marc. (1995). Arthur's TV Trouble
Bullard, Lisa, illustrated by Brian Reibeling. (2003). Marvelous Me: Inside and Out
Carlson, Nancy. L. (1988). I Like Me
Fernandes, Kim and Fernandes, Eugenie. (1997). Little Toby and the Big Hair
hooks, bell, illustrated by Chris Raschka. (1999). Happy to Be Nappy
Hutchins, Pat. (1968). Rosie's Walk
Jones, Carol. (2002). The Gingerbread Man
Ransom, Candice, illustrated by Felicia Bond. (1993). The Big Green Pocketbook
Richmond, Marianne. (2001). Hooray for You
Rosen, Michael, illustrated by Helen Oxenbury. (1989). We're Going on a Bear Hunt
Saltzberg, Barney. (2003). Crazy Hair Day

Lighthouse
Bahr, Mary, illustrated by David Cunningham. (1992). The Memory Box
Barron, T.A., illustrated by Chris K. Soentpiet. (2000). Where Is Grandpa?
Bourgeois, Paulette, illustrated by Stéphane Jorisch. (2001). Oma's Quilt
Bunting, Eve, illustrated by Ted Rand. (1996). Secret Place
Edith Newlin Chase, illustrated by Yolaine Lefebvre. (1996). Secret Dawn
Cooke, Trish, illustrated by Sharon Wilson. (2000). The Grandad Tree

Fox, Mem, illustrated by Julie Vivas. (1985). *Wilfrid Gordon McDonald Partridge*

Galbraith, Kathryn O., illustrated by Floyd Cooper. (1997). *Laura Charlotte*

London, Jonathan, illustrated by Gilles Pelletier. (1995). *The Sugaring-off Party*

Look, Lenore, illustrated by Yumi Heo. (2001). *Henry's First-Moon Birthday*

Sheryl MacFarlane, illustrated by Ron Lightburn. (1991). *Waiting for the Whales*

MacLachlan, Patricia, illustrated by Mike Wimmer. (1994). *All the Places to Love*

Ryan, Pam Muñoz, illustrated by Mary Whyte. (2003). *A Box of Friends*

Rylant, Cynthia, illustrated by Diane Goode. (1982). *When I Was Young in the Mountains*

Rui Umezawa, illustrated by Yuji Ando, *Aiko's Flowers* (1999)

Waboose, Jan Bourdeau, illustrated by C.J. Taylor. (1999). *Firedancers*

Waboose, Jan Bourdeau, illustrated by Karen Reczuch, (1997). *Morning on the Lake*

Wood, Douglas, illustrated by Dan Andreasen. (2002). *A Quiet Place*

No Clean Clothes
Ada, Alma Flor, illustrated by Leslie Tryon. (2001). *With Love, Little Red Hen*

Caseley, Judith. (1991). *Dear Annie*

Durant, Alan, illustrated by Vanessa Cabban. (2004). *Dear Tooth Fairy*

Harrison, Joanna. (1996). *When Mom Turned Into a Monster*

Kelley, True. (2005). *School Lunch*

Sadu, Itah, illustrated by Roy Condy. (1993). *Please Clean Up Your Room!*

Skurzynski, Gloria, illustrated by Lynn Munsinger. (1979). *Martin by Himself*

Teague, Mark. (2002). *Dear Mrs. LaRue*

Viorst, Judith, illustrated by Robin Preiss Glasser. (2001). *Super-Completely and Totally the Messiest*

Wells, Rosemary. (1991). *Fritz and the Mess Fairy*

I'm So Embarrassed!
Bang, Molly. (1999). *When Sophie Gets Angry – Really, Really Angry*

D'Arc, Karen Scourby, illustrated by Dianne Palmisciano. (2001). *My Grandmother Is a Singing Yaya*

Gove, Doris, illustrated by Marilynn H. Mallory. (1999). *My Mother Talks to Trees*

Harper, Jessica, illustrated by Lindsay Harper

DuPont. (2004). *Lizzy's Ups and Downs*

Vail, Rachel, illustrated by Yumi Heo. (2002). *Sometimes I'm Bombaloo*

More Pies!
Goldilocks and the Three Bears

Ehlert, Lois. (2004). *Pie in the Sky*

The Sandcastle Contest
Cooper, Helen, illustrated by Ted Dewan . (2002). *Sandmare*

Lies, Brian. (2001). *Hamlet and the Magnificent Sandcastle*

Mahoney, Daniel J. (2005). *A Really Good Snowman*

Yee, Brenda Shannon, illustrated by Thea Kliros. (1999). *Sand Castle*

Websites

Robert Munsch
http://www.robertmunsch.com
The author's official website.

http://www.scholastic.ca
Check Scholastic Canada's website for more information on Robert Munsch.

Alan and Lea Daniel
http://www.kidscanpress.com
Check under Authors & Illustrators.

Janet Wilson
http://www.kidscanpress.com
Check under Authors & Illustrators.

http://www.canscaip.org/bios/wilsonj.html

http://www.papertigers.org/gallery/index_Wilson.html#

http://www.janetwilson.ca/index.asp
Janet Wilson's own website.

Michael Martchenko
http://www.scholastic.ca
Check Scholastic Canada's website for more information on Michael Martchenko.

http://www.annickpress.com
Check under Authors & Illustrators.

Videos

"The Life and Times of Robert Munsch" (2000) is an episode of CBC television's Life and Times series. It is designed for an adult audience but offers interesting insights into and information about Munsch's life and work. To order, see the CBC website at http://www.cbc.ca

"Meet the Author: Robert Munsch" (1985) is a short video from Mead Educational designed for a children's audience, with information about Munsch's life and work. It is available at most public libraries.

Book and Audio

"Tell Me a Story" Robert Munsch book-and-CD or book-and-cassette packages.

CD

Love You Forever: The Best of Robert Munsch (2003).
Murmel Murmel Munsch: 14 more best-loved stories performed by Robert Munsch (2006). Two of the stories are featured in this guide: *No Clean Clothes* (*Lacey's Kiss* on the CD) and *I'm So Embarrassed!*.

Biography Information

Canadian Children's Book Centre. (1999). *The Storymakers: Illustrating Children's Books.*
Canadian Children's Book Centre. (2000). *The Storymakers: Writing Children's Books.*
Gertridge, Allison. (2002). *Meet Canadian Authors and Illustrators,* Second Edition.
Jones, Raymond and Stott, John. (2000). *Canadian Children's Books: A Critical Guide to Authors and Illustrators.*